50 Fresh and Fruity Smoothie Bowl Recipes for Home

By: Kelly Johnson

Table of Contents

Tropical Bliss Bowl:

- Mango
- Pineapple
- Coconut water
- Banana
- Spinach

Berry Blast Bowl:

- Mixed berries (strawberries, blueberries, raspberries)
- Almond milk
- Chia seeds
- Banana

Peachy Keen Delight:

- Peaches
- Greek yogurt
- Orange juice
- Honey

Green Goddess Bowl:

- Kiwi
- Green apple
- Spinach
- Coconut milk

Dragon Fruit Dream:

- Dragon fruit
- Pineapple
- Coconut water
- Mango

Mango Tango Bowl:

- Mango
- Pineapple
- Greek yogurt
- Orange juice

Blue Lagoon Bowl:

- Blueberries
- Banana
- Almond milk
- Chia seeds

Raspberry Sunshine Bowl:

- Raspberries
- Pineapple
- Coconut water
- Greek yogurt

Citrus Splash Bowl:

- Oranges
- Pineapple
- Banana
- Spinach

Strawberry Fields Forever:

- Strawberries
- Almond milk
- Chia seeds
- Coconut flakes

Kiwi Coconut Crush:

- Kiwi
- Coconut milk
- Banana

- Spinach

Pineapple Paradise Bowl:

- Pineapple
- Mango
- Greek yogurt
- Coconut water

Minty Melon Bowl:

- Watermelon

Tropical Bliss Bowl:

Mango

Ingredients:

- 1 ripe mango, peeled and diced
- 1/2 cup pineapple chunks
- 1/2 cup coconut water
- 1 banana, sliced
- Handful of spinach leaves (optional for added nutrients)

Instructions:

In a blender, combine the diced mango, pineapple chunks, coconut water, banana, and spinach leaves (if using).
Blend until smooth and creamy.
Pour the smoothie into a bowl.
Top with your favorite toppings, such as sliced mango, granola, chia seeds, or shredded coconut.
Enjoy your refreshing Tropical Bliss Bowl!

Feel free to customize this recipe by adding or adjusting ingredients based on your preferences.

Pineapple

Ingredients:

- 1 ripe mango, peeled and diced
- 1 cup pineapple chunks
- 1/2 cup coconut water
- 1 banana, sliced
- Handful of spinach leaves (optional for added nutrients)

Instructions:

In a blender, combine the diced mango, pineapple chunks, coconut water, banana, and spinach leaves (if using).
Blend until smooth and creamy.
Pour the smoothie into a bowl.
Top with additional pineapple chunks, sliced mango, granola, chia seeds, or shredded coconut for added texture and flavor.
Enjoy your Tropical Pineapple Bliss Bowl!

Feel free to adjust the quantities and experiment with different toppings to suit your taste preferences.

Coconut water

Ingredients:

- 1 ripe mango, peeled and diced
- 1 cup pineapple chunks
- 1/2 cup coconut water
- 1 banana, sliced
- Handful of spinach leaves (optional for added nutrients)

Instructions:

In a blender, combine the diced mango, pineapple chunks, coconut water, banana, and spinach leaves (if using).
Blend until smooth and creamy.
Pour the smoothie into a bowl.
Top with additional pineapple chunks, sliced mango, and any desired toppings like granola, chia seeds, or shredded coconut.
Drizzle some extra coconut water over the top for added freshness.
Enjoy your Tropical Pineapple Coconut Bliss Bowl!

This bowl combines the tropical flavors of mango and pineapple with the hydrating touch of coconut water for a delicious and refreshing treat. Customize it to your liking and enjoy!

Banana

Ingredients:

- 1 ripe mango, peeled and diced
- 1 cup pineapple chunks
- 1 banana, sliced
- 1/2 cup coconut water
- Handful of spinach leaves (optional for added nutrients)

Instructions:

In a blender, combine the diced mango, pineapple chunks, banana slices, and coconut water.
Add the spinach leaves if you'd like an extra nutritional boost.
Blend until smooth and creamy.
Pour the smoothie into a bowl.
Top with additional pineapple chunks, sliced mango, banana slices, and any desired toppings such as granola, chia seeds, or shredded coconut.
Drizzle some extra coconut water over the top for added freshness.
Enjoy your Tropical Pineapple Coconut Banana Bliss Bowl!

This version highlights the sweet and creamy texture of banana alongside the tropical flavors of mango and pineapple, creating a delicious and nourishing smoothie bowl.

Customize it to your liking and savor the tropical goodness!

Spinach

Ingredients:

- 1 ripe mango, peeled and diced
- 1 cup pineapple chunks
- 1 banana, sliced
- 1/2 cup coconut water
- Handful of fresh spinach leaves
- Toppings: Sliced kiwi, shredded coconut, chia seeds, and granola

Instructions:

In a blender, combine the diced mango, pineapple chunks, banana slices, coconut water, and fresh spinach leaves.
Blend until the mixture is smooth and has a vibrant green color.
Pour the green smoothie into a bowl.
Top the smoothie bowl with sliced kiwi, shredded coconut, chia seeds, and granola for added texture and flavor.
Drizzle some extra coconut water over the top if desired.
Enjoy your Green Tropical Smoothie Bowl!

This bowl not only incorporates the tropical flavors of mango, pineapple, and banana but also adds the nutritional benefits of fresh spinach. Customize the toppings according to your taste preferences and enjoy a nutritious and delicious green smoothie bowl!

Berry Blast Bowl:

Mixed berries (strawberries, blueberries, raspberries)

Ingredients:

- 1 cup mixed berries (strawberries, blueberries, raspberries)
- 1 banana, sliced
- 1/2 cup almond milk
- 1 tablespoon chia seeds
- Toppings: Sliced strawberries, blueberries, raspberries, granola, and a drizzle of honey

Instructions:

In a blender, combine the mixed berries, sliced banana, almond milk, and chia seeds.
Blend until the mixture is smooth and has a vibrant berry color.
Pour the berry smoothie into a bowl.
Top the smoothie bowl with sliced strawberries, blueberries, raspberries, granola, and drizzle honey over the top for added sweetness.
Enjoy your delicious Berry Blast Bowl!

Feel free to customize this recipe by adding or adjusting ingredients based on your preferences. This bowl is packed with the goodness of mixed berries and offers a delightful combination of flavors and textures.

Almond milk

Ingredients:

- 1 cup mixed berries (strawberries, blueberries, raspberries)
- 1 banana, sliced
- 1/2 cup almond milk
- 1 tablespoon chia seeds
- Toppings: Sliced strawberries, blueberries, raspberries, granola, and a drizzle of honey

Instructions:

In a blender, combine the mixed berries, sliced banana, almond milk, and chia seeds.
Blend until the mixture is smooth and has a vibrant berry color.
Pour the berry-almond smoothie into a bowl.
Top the smoothie bowl with sliced strawberries, blueberries, raspberries, granola, and drizzle honey over the top for added sweetness.
Enjoy your delicious Berry Almond Blast Bowl!

The addition of almond milk not only adds creaminess but also complements the berry flavors. Customize the toppings and quantities based on your preferences, and savor this delightful and nutritious almond-infused berry smoothie bowl.

Chia seeds

Ingredients:

- 1 cup mixed berries (strawberries, blueberries, raspberries)
- 1 banana, sliced
- 1/2 cup almond milk
- 1 tablespoon chia seeds
- Toppings: Sliced strawberries, blueberries, raspberries, granola, and a drizzle of honey

Instructions:

In a blender, combine the mixed berries, sliced banana, almond milk, and chia seeds.
Blend until the mixture is smooth and has a vibrant berry color.
Pour the berry-almond chia smoothie into a bowl.
Top the smoothie bowl with sliced strawberries, blueberries, raspberries, granola, and drizzle honey over the top for added sweetness.
Allow the chia seeds to soak in the smoothie for a few minutes, providing a thicker consistency.
Enjoy your delicious Berry Almond Chia Blast Bowl!

The addition of chia seeds not only adds a delightful crunch but also boosts the nutritional content with fiber and omega-3 fatty acids. Customize the toppings to your liking and relish this wholesome and satisfying berry almond chia smoothie bowl.

Banana

Ingredients:

- 1 cup mixed berries (strawberries, blueberries, raspberries)
- 1 banana, sliced
- 1/2 cup almond milk
- 1 tablespoon chia seeds
- Toppings: Sliced strawberries, blueberries, raspberries, granola, and a drizzle of honey

Instructions:

In a blender, combine the mixed berries, sliced banana, almond milk, and chia seeds.
Blend until the mixture is smooth and has a vibrant berry color.
Pour the berry-almond chia banana smoothie into a bowl.
Top the smoothie bowl with sliced strawberries, blueberries, raspberries, granola, and drizzle honey over the top for added sweetness.
Allow the chia seeds to soak in the smoothie for a few minutes, providing a thicker consistency.
Enjoy your delicious Berry Almond Chia Banana Blast Bowl!

The addition of banana not only enhances the creaminess but also adds a natural sweetness to the smoothie bowl. Customize the toppings to your liking and savor this wholesome and satisfying berry almond chia banana smoothie bowl.

Peachy Keen Delight:

Peaches

Ingredients:

- 2 ripe peaches, pitted and sliced
- 1 banana
- 1/2 cup Greek yogurt
- 1/4 cup orange juice
- 1 tablespoon honey (optional, for added sweetness)

Instructions:

In a blender, combine the sliced peaches, banana, Greek yogurt, and orange juice.
If desired, add honey for additional sweetness.
Blend the ingredients until smooth and creamy.
Pour the peachy delight smoothie into a bowl.
Top with additional peach slices and any other preferred toppings, such as granola or sliced almonds.
Enjoy your Peachy Keen Delight Bowl!

Feel free to customize this recipe by adjusting the quantities or adding toppings according to your taste preferences. The natural sweetness of peaches combined with the creaminess of Greek yogurt makes for a delightful and refreshing smoothie bowl.

Greek yogurt

Ingredients:

- 2 ripe peaches, pitted and sliced
- 1 banana
- 1/2 cup Greek yogurt
- 1/4 cup orange juice
- 1 tablespoon honey (optional, for added sweetness)

Instructions:

In a blender, combine the sliced peaches, banana, Greek yogurt, and orange juice.
If desired, add honey for additional sweetness.
Blend the ingredients until smooth and creamy.
Pour the peachy Greek yogurt delight smoothie into a bowl.
Top with additional peach slices and any other preferred toppings, such as granola or sliced almonds.
Enjoy your Peachy Keen Greek Yogurt Delight Bowl!

The addition of Greek yogurt not only adds creaminess but also provides a good source of protein. Customize the toppings to your liking and relish this Peachy Keen Greek Yogurt Delight Bowl as a nutritious and delicious treat!

Orange juice

Ingredients:

- 2 ripe peaches, pitted and sliced
- 1 banana
- 1/2 cup Greek yogurt
- 1/4 cup orange juice
- 1 tablespoon honey (optional, for added sweetness)

Instructions:

In a blender, combine the sliced peaches, banana, Greek yogurt, orange juice, and honey (if using).
Blend the ingredients until smooth and creamy.
Pour the peachy orange Greek yogurt delight smoothie into a bowl.
Top with additional peach slices and any other preferred toppings, such as granola or sliced almonds.
Enjoy your Peachy Orange Greek Yogurt Delight Bowl!

The addition of orange juice not only enhances the flavor but also adds a refreshing citrus kick to the smoothie bowl. Customize the toppings to your liking and savor this Peachy Orange Greek Yogurt Delight Bowl as a delightful and nutritious breakfast or snack!

Honey

Ingredients:

- 2 ripe peaches, pitted and sliced
- 1 banana
- 1/2 cup Greek yogurt
- 1/4 cup orange juice
- 1 tablespoon honey (adjust to taste)

Instructions:

In a blender, combine the sliced peaches, banana, Greek yogurt, orange juice, and honey.

Adjust the amount of honey to achieve your preferred level of sweetness.
Blend the ingredients until smooth and creamy.
Pour the peachy delight honey smoothie into a bowl.
Top with additional peach slices and any other preferred toppings, such as granola or sliced almonds.
Drizzle a little extra honey over the top for added sweetness, if desired.
Enjoy your Peachy Keen Delight Honey Bowl!

This delightful bowl combines the sweet and juicy flavors of peaches with the creaminess of Greek yogurt, the natural sweetness of honey, and the citrusy kick from orange juice. Customize the toppings and sweetness level to your liking and savor this delicious and refreshing Peachy Keen Delight Honey Bowl!

Green apple

Ingredients:

- 2 ripe peaches, pitted and sliced
- 1 green apple, cored and sliced
- 1 banana
- 1/2 cup Greek yogurt
- 1/4 cup orange juice
- 1 tablespoon honey (adjust to taste)

Instructions:

In a blender, combine the sliced peaches, sliced green apple, banana, Greek yogurt, orange juice, and honey.
Adjust the amount of honey to achieve your preferred level of sweetness.
Blend the ingredients until smooth and creamy.
Pour the peachy green apple delight honey smoothie into a bowl.
Top with additional peach slices and any other preferred toppings, such as granola or sliced almonds.
Drizzle a little extra honey over the top for added sweetness, if desired.
Enjoy your Peachy Green Apple Delight Honey Bowl!

The addition of green apple adds a crisp and tangy flavor to complement the sweetness of peaches and honey. Customize the toppings and sweetness level to suit your taste preferences and enjoy this flavorful and nutritious Peachy Green Apple Delight Honey Bowl!

Spinach

Ingredients:

- 2 ripe peaches, pitted and sliced
- 1 green apple, cored and sliced
- Handful of fresh spinach leaves
- 1 banana
- 1/2 cup Greek yogurt
- 1/4 cup orange juice
- 1 tablespoon honey (adjust to taste)

Instructions:

In a blender, combine the sliced peaches, sliced green apple, fresh spinach leaves, banana, Greek yogurt, orange juice, and honey.
Adjust the amount of honey to achieve your preferred level of sweetness.
Blend the ingredients until smooth and creamy.
Pour the peachy green apple spinach delight honey smoothie into a bowl.
Top with additional peach slices and any other preferred toppings, such as granola or sliced almonds.
Drizzle a little extra honey over the top for added sweetness, if desired.
Enjoy your Peachy Green Apple Spinach Delight Honey Bowl!

Adding spinach not only introduces a boost of nutrients but also enhances the vibrant green color of the smoothie bowl. Customize the toppings and sweetness level to your liking and savor this delicious and nourishing Peachy Green Apple Spinach Delight Honey Bowl!

Coconut milk

Ingredients:

- 2 ripe peaches, pitted and sliced
- 1 green apple, cored and sliced
- Handful of fresh spinach leaves
- 1 banana
- 1/2 cup Greek yogurt
- 1/4 cup orange juice
- 1/4 cup coconut milk
- 1 tablespoon honey (adjust to taste)

Instructions:

In a blender, combine the sliced peaches, sliced green apple, fresh spinach leaves, banana, Greek yogurt, orange juice, coconut milk, and honey.
Adjust the amount of honey to achieve your preferred level of sweetness.
Blend the ingredients until smooth and creamy.
Pour the peachy green apple spinach coconut delight honey smoothie into a bowl.
Top with additional peach slices and any other preferred toppings, such as granola or sliced almonds.
Drizzle a little extra honey over the top for added sweetness, if desired.
Enjoy your Peachy Green Apple Spinach Coconut Delight Honey Bowl!

The addition of coconut milk brings a rich and tropical flavor to the smoothie bowl.

Customize the toppings and sweetness level to suit your taste preferences and enjoy this creamy and nutritious Peachy Green Apple Spinach Coconut Delight Honey Bowl!

Dragon Fruit Dream:

Dragon fruit

Ingredients:

- 2 ripe peaches, pitted and sliced
- 1 green apple, cored and sliced
- Handful of fresh spinach leaves
- 1 banana
- 1/2 cup Greek yogurt
- 1/4 cup orange juice
- 1/4 cup coconut milk
- 1 tablespoon honey (adjust to taste)
- 1/2 cup diced dragon fruit

Instructions:

> In a blender, combine the sliced peaches, sliced green apple, fresh spinach leaves, banana, Greek yogurt, orange juice, coconut milk, and honey.
> Adjust the amount of honey to achieve your preferred level of sweetness.
> Blend the ingredients until smooth and creamy.
> Pour the exotic dragon fruit delight smoothie into a bowl.
> Top with additional peach slices, diced dragon fruit, and any other preferred toppings, such as granola or sliced almonds.
> Drizzle a little extra honey over the top for added sweetness, if desired.
> Enjoy your Exotic Dragon Fruit Delight Bowl!

The addition of dragon fruit not only brings a stunning visual appeal to the bowl but also adds a mildly sweet and unique flavor. Customize the toppings and sweetness level to your liking and enjoy this tropical and nutritious Exotic Dragon Fruit Delight Bowl!

Pineapple

Ingredients:

- 2 ripe peaches, pitted and sliced
- 1 green apple, cored and sliced
- Handful of fresh spinach leaves
- 1 banana
- 1/2 cup Greek yogurt
- 1/4 cup orange juice
- 1/4 cup coconut milk
- 1 tablespoon honey (adjust to taste)
- 1/2 cup diced pineapple

Instructions:

In a blender, combine the sliced peaches, sliced green apple, fresh spinach leaves, banana, Greek yogurt, orange juice, coconut milk, and honey.
Adjust the amount of honey to achieve your preferred level of sweetness.
Blend the ingredients until smooth and creamy.
Pour the tropical pineapple delight smoothie into a bowl.
Top with additional peach slices, diced pineapple, and any other preferred toppings, such as granola or sliced almonds.
Drizzle a little extra honey over the top for added sweetness, if desired.
Enjoy your Tropical Pineapple Delight Bowl!

The addition of pineapple adds a sweet and tropical twist to the smoothie bowl.

Customize the toppings and sweetness level to your liking and savor this refreshing and nutritious Tropical Pineapple Delight Bowl!

Coconut water

Ingredients:

- 2 ripe peaches, pitted and sliced
- 1 green apple, cored and sliced
- Handful of fresh spinach leaves
- 1 banana
- 1/2 cup Greek yogurt
- 1/4 cup orange juice
- 1/4 cup coconut milk
- 1/4 cup coconut water
- 1 tablespoon honey (adjust to taste)

Instructions:

In a blender, combine the sliced peaches, sliced green apple, fresh spinach leaves, banana, Greek yogurt, orange juice, coconut milk, coconut water, and honey.
Adjust the amount of honey to achieve your preferred level of sweetness.
Blend the ingredients until smooth and creamy.
Pour the tropical coconut water delight smoothie into a bowl.
Top with additional peach slices and any other preferred toppings, such as granola or sliced almonds.
Drizzle a little extra honey over the top for added sweetness, if desired.
Enjoy your Tropical Coconut Water Delight Bowl!

The addition of coconut water enhances the overall hydration and provides a light and refreshing element to the smoothie bowl. Customize the toppings and sweetness level to your liking and savor this delicious and tropical Tropical Coconut Water Delight Bowl!

Mango

Ingredients:

- 2 ripe peaches, pitted and sliced
- 1 green apple, cored and sliced
- Handful of fresh spinach leaves
- 1 banana
- 1/2 cup Greek yogurt
- 1/4 cup orange juice
- 1/4 cup coconut milk
- 1/4 cup coconut water
- 1 tablespoon honey (adjust to taste)
- 1/2 cup diced mango

Instructions:

In a blender, combine the sliced peaches, sliced green apple, fresh spinach leaves, banana, Greek yogurt, orange juice, coconut milk, coconut water, and honey.
Adjust the amount of honey to achieve your preferred level of sweetness.
Add the diced mango to the blender.
Blend the ingredients until smooth and creamy.
Pour the mango coconut water delight smoothie into a bowl.
Top with additional peach slices and any other preferred toppings, such as granola or sliced almonds.
Drizzle a little extra honey over the top for added sweetness, if desired.
Enjoy your Mango Coconut Water Delight Bowl!

The addition of mango adds a luscious tropical flavor to the smoothie bowl. Customize the toppings and sweetness level to your liking and savor this delicious and hydrating Mango Coconut Water Delight Bowl!

Mango Tango Bowl:

Mango

Ingredients:

- 2 ripe mangoes, peeled and diced
- 1 banana
- 1/2 cup Greek yogurt
- 1/4 cup orange juice
- 1 tablespoon honey (adjust to taste)
- Toppings: Sliced mango, granola, chia seeds, and a sprinkle of coconut flakes

Instructions:

In a blender, combine the diced mangoes, banana, Greek yogurt, orange juice, and honey.
Adjust the amount of honey to achieve your preferred level of sweetness.
Blend the ingredients until smooth and creamy.
Pour the mango tango smoothie into a bowl.
Top with sliced mango, granola, chia seeds, and a sprinkle of coconut flakes for added texture and flavor.
Drizzle a little extra honey over the top if desired.
Enjoy your Mango Tango Bowl!

This Mango Tango Bowl is a delightful and refreshing way to enjoy the tropical goodness of mango. Customize the toppings and sweetness level according to your preferences and relish this delicious and nutritious mango-infused smoothie bowl!

Pineapple

Ingredients:

- 2 ripe mangoes, peeled and diced
- 1 cup pineapple chunks
- 1 banana
- 1/2 cup Greek yogurt
- 1/4 cup orange juice
- 1 tablespoon honey (adjust to taste)
- Toppings: Sliced mango, pineapple chunks, granola, chia seeds, and a sprinkle of coconut flakes

Instructions:

In a blender, combine the diced mangoes, pineapple chunks, banana, Greek yogurt, orange juice, and honey.
Adjust the amount of honey to achieve your preferred level of sweetness.
Blend the ingredients until smooth and creamy.
Pour the mango pineapple tango smoothie into a bowl.
Top with sliced mango, additional pineapple chunks, granola, chia seeds, and a sprinkle of coconut flakes for added texture and flavor.
Drizzle a little extra honey over the top if desired.
Enjoy your Mango Pineapple Tango Bowl!

The addition of pineapple brings a sweet and tangy element to the bowl, complementing the tropical flavors of mango. Customize the toppings and sweetness level according to your liking and savor this delicious and nutritious Mango Pineapple Tango Bowl!

Greek yogurt

Ingredients:

- 2 ripe mangoes, peeled and diced
- 1 cup pineapple chunks
- 1 banana
- 1/2 cup Greek yogurt
- 1/4 cup orange juice
- 1 tablespoon honey (adjust to taste)
- Toppings: Sliced mango, additional pineapple chunks, granola, chia seeds, and a sprinkle of coconut flakes

Instructions:

In a blender, combine the diced mangoes, pineapple chunks, banana, Greek yogurt, orange juice, and honey.
Adjust the amount of honey to achieve your preferred level of sweetness.
Blend the ingredients until smooth and creamy.
Pour the mango pineapple Greek yogurt tango smoothie into a bowl.
Top with sliced mango, additional pineapple chunks, granola, chia seeds, and a sprinkle of coconut flakes for added texture and flavor.
Drizzle a little extra honey over the top if desired.
Enjoy your Mango Pineapple Greek Yogurt Tango Bowl!

The addition of Greek yogurt not only provides creaminess but also adds a protein boost to make this smoothie bowl more satisfying. Customize the toppings and sweetness level according to your liking and relish this delicious and protein-packed Mango Pineapple Greek Yogurt Tango Bowl!

Orange juice

Ingredients:

- 2 ripe mangoes, peeled and diced
- 1 cup pineapple chunks
- 1 banana
- 1/2 cup Greek yogurt
- 1/4 cup orange juice
- 1 tablespoon honey (adjust to taste)
- Toppings: Sliced mango, additional pineapple chunks, granola, chia seeds, and a sprinkle of coconut flakes

Instructions:

In a blender, combine the diced mangoes, pineapple chunks, banana, Greek yogurt, orange juice, and honey.
Adjust the amount of honey to achieve your preferred level of sweetness.
Blend the ingredients until smooth and creamy.
Pour the citrus mango pineapple Greek yogurt tango smoothie into a bowl.
Top with sliced mango, additional pineapple chunks, granola, chia seeds, and a sprinkle of coconut flakes for added texture and flavor.
Drizzle a little extra honey over the top if desired.
Enjoy your Citrus Mango Pineapple Greek Yogurt Tango Bowl!

The addition of orange juice adds a delightful citrus kick, enhancing the overall flavor profile of this refreshing smoothie bowl. Customize the toppings and sweetness level according to your liking and savor this delicious and citrusy Mango Pineapple Greek Yogurt Tango Bowl!

Blue Lagoon Bowl:

Blueberries

Ingredients:

- 1 cup blueberries (fresh or frozen)
- 1 banana
- 1/2 cup Greek yogurt
- 1/4 cup almond milk
- 1 tablespoon chia seeds
- Toppings: Additional blueberries, sliced banana, granola, and a drizzle of honey

Instructions:

In a blender, combine the blueberries, banana, Greek yogurt, almond milk, and chia seeds.
Blend the ingredients until smooth and creamy.
Pour the blue lagoon smoothie into a bowl.
Top with additional blueberries, sliced banana, granola, and a drizzle of honey for added sweetness.
Enjoy your Blue Lagoon Bowl!

This bowl celebrates the vibrant and antioxidant-rich blueberries, providing a delicious and nutritious treat. Customize the toppings and sweetness level according to your preferences, and relish the refreshing flavors of the Blue Lagoon Bowl!

Banana

Ingredients:

- 1 cup blueberries (fresh or frozen)
- 1 banana
- 1/2 cup Greek yogurt
- 1/4 cup almond milk
- 1 tablespoon chia seeds
- Toppings: Additional blueberries, sliced banana, granola, and a drizzle of honey

Instructions:

In a blender, combine the blueberries, banana, Greek yogurt, almond milk, and chia seeds.
Blend the ingredients until smooth and creamy.
Pour the blueberry banana lagoon smoothie into a bowl.
Top with additional blueberries, sliced banana, granola, and a drizzle of honey for added sweetness.
Enjoy your Blueberry Banana Lagoon Bowl!

The addition of banana not only enhances the creaminess of the smoothie but also adds natural sweetness. Customize the toppings and sweetness level according to your liking and enjoy this delicious and nutritious Blueberry Banana Lagoon Bowl!

Almond milk

Ingredients:

- 1 cup blueberries (fresh or frozen)
- 1 banana
- 1/2 cup Greek yogurt
- 1/4 cup almond milk
- 1 tablespoon chia seeds
- Toppings: Additional blueberries, sliced banana, granola, and a drizzle of honey

Instructions:

In a blender, combine the blueberries, banana, Greek yogurt, almond milk, and chia seeds.
Blend the ingredients until smooth and creamy.
Pour the blueberry banana almond lagoon smoothie into a bowl.
Top with additional blueberries, sliced banana, granola, and a drizzle of honey for added sweetness.
Enjoy your Blueberry Banana Almond Lagoon Bowl!

The addition of almond milk brings a nutty flavor and creamy consistency to the smoothie bowl. Customize the toppings and sweetness level according to your preferences, and savor the delicious combination of blueberries, banana, and almond in this Blueberry Banana Almond Lagoon Bowl!

Chia seeds

Ingredients:

- 1 cup blueberries (fresh or frozen)
- 1 banana
- 1/2 cup Greek yogurt
- 1/4 cup almond milk
- 1 tablespoon chia seeds
- Toppings: Additional blueberries, sliced banana, granola, and a drizzle of honey

Instructions:

In a blender, combine the blueberries, banana, Greek yogurt, almond milk, and chia seeds.
Blend the ingredients until smooth and creamy.
Pour the blueberry banana almond chia lagoon smoothie into a bowl.
Top with additional blueberries, sliced banana, granola, and a drizzle of honey for added sweetness.
Allow the chia seeds to soak in the smoothie for a few minutes, providing a thicker consistency.
Enjoy your Blueberry Banana Almond Chia Lagoon Bowl!

The addition of chia seeds not only adds a delightful crunch but also boosts the nutritional content with fiber and omega-3 fatty acids. Customize the toppings and sweetness level to your liking and savor this delicious and nutritious Blueberry Banana Almond Chia Lagoon Bowl!

Raspberry Sunshine Bowl:

Raspberries

Ingredients:

- 1 cup raspberries (fresh or frozen)
- 1 banana
- 1/2 cup Greek yogurt
- 1/4 cup orange juice
- 1 tablespoon honey (adjust to taste)
- Toppings: Additional raspberries, sliced banana, granola, and a sprinkle of sliced almonds

Instructions:

In a blender, combine the raspberries, banana, Greek yogurt, orange juice, and honey.
Adjust the amount of honey to achieve your preferred level of sweetness.
Blend the ingredients until smooth and creamy.
Pour the raspberry sunshine smoothie into a bowl.
Top with additional raspberries, sliced banana, granola, and a sprinkle of sliced almonds for added texture.
Drizzle a little extra honey over the top if desired.
Enjoy your Raspberry Sunshine Bowl!

This bowl celebrates the sweet and tangy flavor of raspberries, creating a delicious and refreshing smoothie bowl. Customize the toppings and sweetness level according to your preferences, and relish the vibrant Raspberry Sunshine Bowl!

Pineapple

Ingredients:

- 1 cup raspberries (fresh or frozen)
- 1/2 cup pineapple chunks
- 1 banana
- 1/2 cup Greek yogurt
- 1/4 cup orange juice
- 1 tablespoon honey (adjust to taste)
- Toppings: Additional raspberries, pineapple chunks, sliced banana, granola, and a sprinkle of sliced almonds

Instructions:

In a blender, combine the raspberries, pineapple chunks, banana, Greek yogurt, orange juice, and honey.
Adjust the amount of honey to achieve your preferred level of sweetness.
Blend the ingredients until smooth and creamy.
Pour the tropical raspberry sunshine smoothie into a bowl.
Top with additional raspberries, pineapple chunks, sliced banana, granola, and a sprinkle of sliced almonds for added texture.
Drizzle a little extra honey over the top if desired.
Enjoy your Tropical Raspberry Sunshine Bowl!

The addition of pineapple brings a sweet and tropical element to the bowl, complementing the tangy raspberries. Customize the toppings and sweetness level according to your liking and savor this delicious and tropical Tropical Raspberry Sunshine Bowl!

Coconut water

Ingredients:

- 1 cup raspberries (fresh or frozen)
- 1/2 cup pineapple chunks
- 1 banana
- 1/2 cup Greek yogurt
- 1/4 cup orange juice
- 1/4 cup coconut water
- 1 tablespoon honey (adjust to taste)
- Toppings: Additional raspberries, pineapple chunks, sliced banana, granola, and a sprinkle of sliced almonds

Instructions:

In a blender, combine the raspberries, pineapple chunks, banana, Greek yogurt, orange juice, coconut water, and honey.
Adjust the amount of honey to achieve your preferred level of sweetness.
Blend the ingredients until smooth and creamy.
Pour the hydrating tropical raspberry sunshine smoothie into a bowl.
Top with additional raspberries, pineapple chunks, sliced banana, granola, and a sprinkle of sliced almonds for added texture.
Drizzle a little extra honey over the top if desired.
Enjoy your Hydrating Tropical Raspberry Sunshine Bowl!

The addition of coconut water provides a light and refreshing element to the smoothie bowl. Customize the toppings and sweetness level according to your liking and savor this delicious and hydrating Hydrating Tropical Raspberry Sunshine Bowl!

Greek yogurt

Ingredients:

- 1 cup raspberries (fresh or frozen)
- 1/2 cup pineapple chunks
- 1 banana
- 1/2 cup Greek yogurt
- 1/4 cup orange juice
- 1/4 cup coconut water
- 1 tablespoon honey (adjust to taste)
- Toppings: Additional raspberries, pineapple chunks, sliced banana, granola, and a sprinkle of sliced almonds

Instructions:

In a blender, combine the raspberries, pineapple chunks, banana, Greek yogurt, orange juice, coconut water, and honey.
Adjust the amount of honey to achieve your preferred level of sweetness.
Blend the ingredients until smooth and creamy.
Pour the protein-packed tropical raspberry sunshine smoothie into a bowl.
Top with additional raspberries, pineapple chunks, sliced banana, granola, and a sprinkle of sliced almonds for added texture.
Drizzle a little extra honey over the top if desired.
Enjoy your Protein-Packed Tropical Raspberry Sunshine Bowl!

The addition of Greek yogurt not only enhances the creaminess but also provides a protein boost, making this smoothie bowl more satisfying. Customize the toppings and sweetness level according to your liking and savor this delicious and protein-packed Protein-Packed Tropical Raspberry Sunshine Bowl!

Citrus Splash Bowl:

Oranges

Ingredients:

- 1 cup oranges, peeled and segmented
- 1 banana
- 1/2 cup Greek yogurt
- 1/4 cup orange juice
- 1 tablespoon honey (adjust to taste)
- Toppings: Additional orange segments, sliced banana, granola, and a sprinkle of chopped pistachios

Instructions:

In a blender, combine the oranges, banana, Greek yogurt, orange juice, and honey.
Adjust the amount of honey to achieve your preferred level of sweetness.
Blend the ingredients until smooth and creamy.
Pour the citrus splash smoothie into a bowl.
Top with additional orange segments, sliced banana, granola, and a sprinkle of chopped pistachios for added texture.
Drizzle a little extra honey over the top if desired.
Enjoy your Citrus Splash Bowl!

This bowl celebrates the vibrant and citrusy flavor of oranges, creating a delicious and refreshing smoothie bowl. Customize the toppings and sweetness level according to your preferences, and relish the zesty Citrus Splash Bowl!

Pineapple

Ingredients:

- 1 cup oranges, peeled and segmented
- 1/2 cup pineapple chunks
- 1 banana
- 1/2 cup Greek yogurt
- 1/4 cup orange juice
- 1 tablespoon honey (adjust to taste)
- Toppings: Additional orange segments, pineapple chunks, sliced banana, granola, and a sprinkle of chopped pistachios

Instructions:

In a blender, combine the oranges, pineapple chunks, banana, Greek yogurt, orange juice, and honey.
Adjust the amount of honey to achieve your preferred level of sweetness.
Blend the ingredients until smooth and creamy.
Pour the tropical citrus splash smoothie into a bowl.
Top with additional orange segments, pineapple chunks, sliced banana, granola, and a sprinkle of chopped pistachios for added texture.
Drizzle a little extra honey over the top if desired.
Enjoy your Tropical Citrus Splash Bowl!

The addition of pineapple brings a sweet and tropical element to the bowl, complementing the citrusy flavors of oranges. Customize the toppings and sweetness level according to your liking and savor this delicious and tropical Tropical Citrus Splash Bowl!

Banana

Ingredients:

- 1 cup oranges, peeled and segmented
- 1/2 cup pineapple chunks
- 1 banana
- 1/2 cup Greek yogurt
- 1/4 cup orange juice
- 1 tablespoon honey (adjust to taste)
- Toppings: Additional orange segments, pineapple chunks, sliced banana, granola, and a sprinkle of chopped pistachios

Instructions:

In a blender, combine the oranges, pineapple chunks, banana, Greek yogurt, orange juice, and honey.
Adjust the amount of honey to achieve your preferred level of sweetness.
Blend the ingredients until smooth and creamy.
Pour the banana citrus splash smoothie into a bowl.
Top with additional orange segments, pineapple chunks, sliced banana, granola, and a sprinkle of chopped pistachios for added texture.
Drizzle a little extra honey over the top if desired.
Enjoy your Banana Citrus Splash Bowl!

The addition of banana not only enhances the creaminess of the smoothie but also adds a natural sweetness. Customize the toppings and sweetness level according to your liking and savor this delicious and tropical Banana Citrus Splash Bowl!

Spinach

Ingredients:

- 1 cup oranges, peeled and segmented
- 1/2 cup pineapple chunks
- 1 banana
- Handful of fresh spinach leaves
- 1/2 cup Greek yogurt
- 1/4 cup orange juice
- 1 tablespoon honey (adjust to taste)
- Toppings: Additional orange segments, pineapple chunks, sliced banana, granola, and a sprinkle of chopped pistachios

Instructions:

In a blender, combine the oranges, pineapple chunks, banana, fresh spinach leaves, Greek yogurt, orange juice, and honey.
Adjust the amount of honey to achieve your preferred level of sweetness.
Blend the ingredients until smooth and creamy.
Pour the green citrus splash smoothie into a bowl.
Top with additional orange segments, pineapple chunks, sliced banana, granola, and a sprinkle of chopped pistachios for added texture.
Drizzle a little extra honey over the top if desired.
Enjoy your Green Citrus Splash Bowl!

The addition of spinach not only adds nutritional value but also creates a beautiful green hue in the smoothie bowl. Customize the toppings and sweetness level according to your liking and savor this delicious and vibrant Green Citrus Splash Bowl!

Strawberry Fields Forever:

Strawberries

Ingredients:

- 1 cup oranges, peeled and segmented
- 1/2 cup pineapple chunks
- 1 banana
- Handful of fresh spinach leaves
- 1/2 cup Greek yogurt
- 1/4 cup orange juice
- 1 tablespoon honey (adjust to taste)
- 1/2 cup strawberries, hulled and halved
- Toppings: Additional orange segments, pineapple chunks, sliced banana, sliced strawberries, granola, and a sprinkle of chopped pistachios

Instructions:

> In a blender, combine the oranges, pineapple chunks, banana, fresh spinach leaves, Greek yogurt, orange juice, and honey.
> Adjust the amount of honey to achieve your preferred level of sweetness.
> Add the strawberries to the blender.
> Blend the ingredients until smooth and creamy.
> Pour the berry citrus splash smoothie into a bowl.
> Top with additional orange segments, pineapple chunks, sliced banana, sliced strawberries, granola, and a sprinkle of chopped pistachios for added texture.
> Drizzle a little extra honey over the top if desired.
> Enjoy your Berry Citrus Splash Bowl!

The addition of strawberries brings a delightful sweetness and vibrant color to the bowl.

Customize the toppings and sweetness level according to your liking and savor this delicious and colorful Berry Citrus Splash Bowl!

Almond milk

Ingredients:

- 1 cup oranges, peeled and segmented
- 1/2 cup pineapple chunks
- 1 banana
- Handful of fresh spinach leaves
- 1/2 cup Greek yogurt
- 1/4 cup orange juice
- 1/4 cup almond milk
- 1 tablespoon honey (adjust to taste)
- 1/2 cup strawberries, hulled and halved
- Toppings: Additional orange segments, pineapple chunks, sliced banana, sliced strawberries, granola, and a sprinkle of chopped pistachios

Instructions:

In a blender, combine the oranges, pineapple chunks, banana, fresh spinach leaves, Greek yogurt, orange juice, almond milk, and honey.
Adjust the amount of honey to achieve your preferred level of sweetness.
Add the strawberries to the blender.
Blend the ingredients until smooth and creamy.
Pour the nutty berry citrus splash smoothie into a bowl.
Top with additional orange segments, pineapple chunks, sliced banana, sliced strawberries, granola, and a sprinkle of chopped pistachios for added texture.
Drizzle a little extra honey over the top if desired.
Enjoy your Nutty Berry Citrus Splash Bowl!

The addition of almond milk brings a nutty and creamy element to the smoothie bowl. Customize the toppings and sweetness level according to your liking and savor this delicious and nutrient-packed Nutty Berry Citrus Splash Bowl!

Chia seeds

Ingredients:

- 1 cup oranges, peeled and segmented
- 1/2 cup pineapple chunks
- 1 banana
- Handful of fresh spinach leaves
- 1/2 cup Greek yogurt
- 1/4 cup orange juice
- 1/4 cup almond milk
- 1 tablespoon chia seeds
- 1 tablespoon honey (adjust to taste)
- 1/2 cup strawberries, hulled and halved
- Toppings: Additional orange segments, pineapple chunks, sliced banana, sliced strawberries, granola, and a sprinkle of chopped pistachios

Instructions:

In a blender, combine the oranges, pineapple chunks, banana, fresh spinach leaves, Greek yogurt, orange juice, almond milk, chia seeds, and honey.
Adjust the amount of honey to achieve your preferred level of sweetness.
Add the strawberries to the blender.
Blend the ingredients until smooth and creamy.
Pour the chia berry citrus splash smoothie into a bowl.
Top with additional orange segments, pineapple chunks, sliced banana, sliced strawberries, granola, and a sprinkle of chopped pistachios for added texture.
Drizzle a little extra honey over the top if desired.
Enjoy your Chia Berry Citrus Splash Bowl!

The addition of chia seeds not only adds a delightful crunch but also boosts the nutritional content with fiber and omega-3 fatty acids. Customize the toppings and sweetness level according to your liking and savor this delicious and nutrient-packed Chia Berry Citrus Splash Bowl!

Coconut flakes

Ingredients:

- 1 cup oranges, peeled and segmented
- 1/2 cup pineapple chunks
- 1 banana
- Handful of fresh spinach leaves
- 1/2 cup Greek yogurt
- 1/4 cup orange juice
- 1/4 cup almond milk
- 1 tablespoon chia seeds
- 1 tablespoon honey (adjust to taste)
- 1/2 cup strawberries, hulled and halved
- Toppings: Additional orange segments, pineapple chunks, sliced banana, sliced strawberries, granola, a sprinkle of chopped pistachios, and coconut flakes

Instructions:

In a blender, combine the oranges, pineapple chunks, banana, fresh spinach leaves, Greek yogurt, orange juice, almond milk, chia seeds, and honey.
Adjust the amount of honey to achieve your preferred level of sweetness.
Add the strawberries to the blender.
Blend the ingredients until smooth and creamy.
Pour the tropical chia berry citrus splash smoothie into a bowl.
Top with additional orange segments, pineapple chunks, sliced banana, sliced strawberries, granola, a sprinkle of chopped pistachios, and coconut flakes for added texture.
Drizzle a little extra honey over the top if desired.
Enjoy your Tropical Chia Berry Citrus Splash Bowl!

The addition of coconut flakes brings a tropical and crunchy element to the smoothie bowl. Customize the toppings and sweetness level according to your liking and savor this delicious and texture-rich Tropical Chia Berry Citrus Splash Bowl!

Kiwi Coconut Crush:

Kiwi

Ingredients:

- 2 kiwis, peeled and sliced
- 1/2 cup pineapple chunks
- 1 banana
- 1/2 cup Greek yogurt
- 1/4 cup coconut milk
- 1 tablespoon honey (adjust to taste)
- Toppings: Additional kiwi slices, pineapple chunks, sliced banana, granola, and shredded coconut

Instructions:

In a blender, combine the sliced kiwis, pineapple chunks, banana, Greek yogurt, coconut milk, and honey.
Adjust the amount of honey to achieve your preferred level of sweetness.
Blend the ingredients until smooth and creamy.
Pour the kiwi coconut crush smoothie into a bowl.
Top with additional kiwi slices, pineapple chunks, sliced banana, granola, and shredded coconut for added texture.
Drizzle a little extra honey over the top if desired.
Enjoy your Kiwi Coconut Crush Bowl!

This bowl celebrates the tropical and tangy flavor of kiwi, combined with the creamy texture of coconut. Customize the toppings and sweetness level according to your preferences, and relish the delightful Kiwi Coconut Crush Bowl!

Coconut milk

Ingredients:

- 2 kiwis, peeled and sliced
- 1/2 cup pineapple chunks
- 1 banana
- 1/2 cup Greek yogurt
- 1/4 cup coconut milk
- 1 tablespoon honey (adjust to taste)
- Toppings: Additional kiwi slices, pineapple chunks, sliced banana, granola, and shredded coconut

Instructions:

In a blender, combine the sliced kiwis, pineapple chunks, banana, Greek yogurt, coconut milk, and honey.
Adjust the amount of honey to achieve your preferred level of sweetness.
Blend the ingredients until smooth and creamy.
Pour the creamy kiwi coconut crush smoothie into a bowl.
Top with additional kiwi slices, pineapple chunks, sliced banana, granola, and shredded coconut for added texture.
Drizzle a little extra honey over the top if desired.
Enjoy your Creamy Kiwi Coconut Crush Bowl!

The addition of coconut milk brings a rich and creamy texture to the smoothie bowl, complementing the tropical flavors of kiwi. Customize the toppings and sweetness level according to your liking and savor this indulgent and delicious Creamy Kiwi Coconut Crush Bowl!

Banana

Ingredients:

- 2 kiwis, peeled and sliced
- 1/2 cup pineapple chunks
- 1 banana
- 1/2 cup Greek yogurt
- 1/4 cup coconut milk
- 1 tablespoon honey (adjust to taste)
- Toppings: Additional kiwi slices, pineapple chunks, sliced banana, granola, and shredded coconut

Instructions:

In a blender, combine the sliced kiwis, pineapple chunks, banana, Greek yogurt, coconut milk, and honey.
Adjust the amount of honey to achieve your preferred level of sweetness.
Blend the ingredients until smooth and creamy.
Pour the creamy kiwi banana coconut crush smoothie into a bowl.
Top with additional kiwi slices, pineapple chunks, sliced banana, granola, and shredded coconut for added texture.
Drizzle a little extra honey over the top if desired.
Enjoy your Creamy Kiwi Banana Coconut Crush Bowl!

The addition of banana not only enhances the creaminess of the smoothie but also adds natural sweetness. Customize the toppings and sweetness level according to your liking and savor this delicious and tropical Creamy Kiwi Banana Coconut Crush Bowl!

Spinach

Ingredients:

- 2 kiwis, peeled and sliced
- 1/2 cup pineapple chunks
- 1 banana
- Handful of fresh spinach leaves
- 1/2 cup Greek yogurt
- 1/4 cup coconut milk
- 1 tablespoon honey (adjust to taste)
- Toppings: Additional kiwi slices, pineapple chunks, sliced banana, granola, and shredded coconut

Instructions:

In a blender, combine the sliced kiwis, pineapple chunks, banana, fresh spinach leaves, Greek yogurt, coconut milk, and honey.
Adjust the amount of honey to achieve your preferred level of sweetness.
Blend the ingredients until smooth and creamy.
Pour the green kiwi banana coconut crush smoothie into a bowl.
Top with additional kiwi slices, pineapple chunks, sliced banana, granola, and shredded coconut for added texture.
Drizzle a little extra honey over the top if desired.
Enjoy your Green Kiwi Banana Coconut Crush Bowl!

The addition of spinach not only provides a nutritional boost but also gives a vibrant green color to the smoothie bowl. Customize the toppings and sweetness level according to your liking and savor this delicious and nutrient-packed Green Kiwi Banana Coconut Crush Bowl!

Pineapple Paradise Bowl:

Pineapple

Ingredients:

- 1 cup pineapple chunks
- 1 banana
- 1/2 cup Greek yogurt
- 1/4 cup coconut milk
- 1 tablespoon honey (adjust to taste)
- Toppings: Additional pineapple chunks, sliced banana, shredded coconut, granola, and a sprinkle of chia seeds

Instructions:

In a blender, combine the pineapple chunks, banana, Greek yogurt, coconut milk, and honey.
Adjust the amount of honey to achieve your preferred level of sweetness.
Blend the ingredients until smooth and creamy.
Pour the pineapple paradise smoothie into a bowl.
Top with additional pineapple chunks, sliced banana, shredded coconut, granola, and a sprinkle of chia seeds for added texture and nutrition.
Drizzle a little extra honey over the top if desired.
Enjoy your Pineapple Paradise Bowl!

This bowl celebrates the sweet and tropical flavor of pineapple, creating a refreshing and delightful smoothie bowl. Customize the toppings and sweetness level according to your preferences, and relish the tropical Pineapple Paradise Bowl!

Mango

Ingredients:

- 1 cup pineapple chunks
- 1/2 cup mango chunks
- 1 banana
- 1/2 cup Greek yogurt
- 1/4 cup coconut milk
- 1 tablespoon honey (adjust to taste)
- Toppings: Additional pineapple chunks, mango chunks, sliced banana, shredded coconut, granola, and a sprinkle of chia seeds

Instructions:

In a blender, combine the pineapple chunks, mango chunks, banana, Greek yogurt, coconut milk, and honey.
Adjust the amount of honey to achieve your preferred level of sweetness.
Blend the ingredients until smooth and creamy.
Pour the tropical mango pineapple paradise smoothie into a bowl.
Top with additional pineapple chunks, mango chunks, sliced banana, shredded coconut, granola, and a sprinkle of chia seeds for added texture and nutrition.
Drizzle a little extra honey over the top if desired.
Enjoy your Tropical Mango Pineapple Paradise Bowl!

The addition of mango brings a luscious and sweet flavor to complement the pineapple, creating a truly tropical experience. Customize the toppings and sweetness level according to your liking and savor the delicious Tropical Mango Pineapple Paradise Bowl!

Greek yogurt

Ingredients:

- 1 cup pineapple chunks
- 1/2 cup mango chunks
- 1 banana
- 1/2 cup Greek yogurt
- 1/4 cup coconut milk
- 1 tablespoon honey (adjust to taste)
- Toppings: Additional pineapple chunks, mango chunks, sliced banana, shredded coconut, granola, and a sprinkle of chia seeds

Instructions:

In a blender, combine the pineapple chunks, mango chunks, banana, Greek yogurt, coconut milk, and honey.
Adjust the amount of honey to achieve your preferred level of sweetness.
Blend the ingredients until smooth and creamy.
Pour the creamy tropical mango pineapple paradise smoothie into a bowl.
Top with additional pineapple chunks, mango chunks, sliced banana, shredded coconut, granola, and a sprinkle of chia seeds for added texture and nutrition.
Drizzle a little extra honey over the top if desired.
Enjoy your Creamy Tropical Mango Pineapple Paradise Bowl!

The addition of Greek yogurt not only enhances the creaminess but also provides a protein boost, making this smoothie bowl more satisfying. Customize the toppings and sweetness level according to your liking and savor this delicious and protein-packed Creamy Tropical Mango Pineapple Paradise Bowl!

Coconut water

Ingredients:

- 1 cup pineapple chunks
- 1/2 cup mango chunks
- 1 banana
- 1/2 cup Greek yogurt
- 1/4 cup coconut milk
- 1/4 cup coconut water
- 1 tablespoon honey (adjust to taste)
- Toppings: Additional pineapple chunks, mango chunks, sliced banana, shredded coconut, granola, and a sprinkle of chia seeds

Instructions:

In a blender, combine the pineapple chunks, mango chunks, banana, Greek yogurt, coconut milk, coconut water, and honey.
Adjust the amount of honey to achieve your preferred level of sweetness.
Blend the ingredients until smooth and creamy.
Pour the refreshing pineapple paradise smoothie into a bowl.
Top with additional pineapple chunks, mango chunks, sliced banana, shredded coconut, granola, and a sprinkle of chia seeds for added texture and nutrition.
Drizzle a little extra honey over the top if desired.
Enjoy your Refreshing Pineapple Paradise Bowl!

The addition of coconut water adds a light and hydrating element to the smoothie bowl.

Customize the toppings and sweetness level according to your liking and savor this delicious and refreshing Refreshing Pineapple Paradise Bowl!

Minty Melon Bowl:

Watermelon

Ingredients:

- 2 cups watermelon, cubed
- 1 cup cantaloupe, cubed
- 1/2 cup honeydew melon, cubed
- 1 banana
- 1/2 cup Greek yogurt
- 1 tablespoon honey (adjust to taste)
- Fresh mint leaves for garnish
- Toppings: Sliced strawberries, blueberries, granola, and a sprinkle of chia seeds

Instructions:

In a blender, combine the watermelon, cantaloupe, banana, Greek yogurt, and honey.
Adjust the amount of honey to achieve your preferred level of sweetness.
Blend the ingredients until smooth and creamy.
Pour the minty melon smoothie into a bowl.
Top with additional cantaloupe and honeydew melon cubes, sliced strawberries, blueberries, granola, and a sprinkle of chia seeds for added texture.
Garnish with fresh mint leaves for a burst of flavor.
Drizzle a little extra honey over the top if desired.
Enjoy your Minty Melon Bowl!

The addition of mint adds a delightful and refreshing twist to this melon bowl. Customize the toppings and sweetness level according to your liking and savor the Minty Melon Bowl!